Zapier for Automation:

A Professional's Guide to Streamlining Workflows

Introduction

Why Automation Matters in 2025

In today's fast-paced digital world, efficiency is no longer a luxury—it's a necessity. Businesses and professionals are constantly seeking ways to optimize their workflows, reduce manual tasks, and focus on high-impact activities. Automation has emerged as the key driver of productivity, allowing individuals and teams to work smarter, not harder.

With the rise of artificial intelligence (AI), no-code platforms, and cloud-based applications, automation has become more accessible than ever before. What once required expensive software and dedicated developers can now be achieved with just a few clicks. **Zapier** stands at the forefront of this automation revolution, enabling professionals to connect their favorite apps and create seamless workflows without any coding knowledge.

In **2025**, automation is no longer just about convenience—it's about staying competitive. Companies that embrace workflow automation gain a significant edge by:

- **Saving Time** – Automate repetitive tasks and free up hours of manual work.
- **Reducing Errors** – Minimize human mistakes by setting up reliable, rule-based automations.
- **Boosting Productivity** – Allow teams to focus on creative, strategic, and high-value work.
- **Improving Customer Experience** – Respond faster, personalize interactions, and enhance service quality.
- **Enhancing Collaboration** – Sync data across platforms, ensuring smooth communication between departments.

Whether you're a solo entrepreneur looking to automate client follow-ups, a marketing team streamlining social media posts, or an IT professional integrating multiple tools, **Zapier provides the ultimate automation solution**—without the complexity of coding.

What is Zapier? (Overview & Core Features)

Zapier is a **no-code automation platform** that connects thousands of apps, enabling users to create custom workflows known as **Zaps**. These Zaps allow information to flow between different tools automatically, eliminating manual tasks and streamlining processes.

At its core, Zapier works on a simple **Trigger-Action** mechanism:

Trigger: An event that starts the workflow (e.g., receiving a new email, adding a row in a spreadsheet, getting a new form submission).
Action: The task that follows the trigger (e.g., sending a Slack notification, updating a CRM, posting on social media).

Key Features of Zapier:

- **Multi-Step Zaps** – Automate complex workflows with multiple steps.

- **Paths & Conditional Logic** – Create "if this, then that" rules for smarter automation.
- **Webhooks & API Integrations** – Connect apps even if they don't have built-in Zapier support.
- **Data Formatting & Filters** – Modify, clean, and process data automatically.
- **Scheduled & Delayed Actions** – Set specific times for workflows to run.

With **over 6,000+ supported apps**, including Google Workspace, Slack, Trello, HubSpot, Shopify, Notion, and many more, **Zapier can connect virtually any business tool**—making it an essential platform for professionals across industries.

Who This Guide is For

This book is designed for **business professionals** who want to **optimize their workflows, automate repetitive tasks, and enhance efficiency without writing a single line of code**. Whether you're new to automation or looking to take your workflows to the next level, this guide provides actionable insights tailored to different roles:

- ✓ **Business Owners & Entrepreneurs** – Automate invoicing, email marketing, and customer relationship management to save time and focus on growth.
- ✓ **Marketers & Social Media Managers** – Streamline lead generation, content distribution, and social media scheduling to maximize engagement.
- ✓ **Freelancers & Consultants** – Set up client onboarding, invoice reminders, and project tracking systems for seamless business management.
- ✓ **IT & Developers** – Leverage advanced integrations, webhooks, and API connections to create custom automation workflows.
- ✓ **HR & Recruiters** – Automate candidate screening, employee onboarding, and performance tracking to improve HR efficiency.
- ✓ **E-commerce & Sales Teams** – Sync orders, automate follow-ups, and streamline inventory management to boost customer satisfaction.

If you're looking for **practical, real-world automation solutions** that can transform the way you work, this book is for you.

How to Use This Book

This guide is structured to take you from **Zapier beginner to automation expert**. You can follow it **step-by-step** or jump to specific sections based on your needs.

- ➢ **Chapter 1: Getting Started with Zapier** – Understand the fundamentals, set up your account, and create your first automation.
- ➢ **Chapter 2: Essential Zaps for Professionals** – Explore ready-to-use automation templates for different industries and job roles.
- ➢ **Chapter 3: Advanced Zapier Workflows** – Learn about multi-step Zaps, conditional logic, and API integrations for deeper automation.
- ➢ **Chapter 4: Industry-Specific Use Cases** – See real-world examples tailored for business owners, marketers, HR teams, IT professionals, and more.

➢ **Chapter 5: Troubleshooting & Optimization** – Discover how to debug failed Zaps, optimize performance, and reduce automation costs.

➢ **Chapter 6: Future Trends in Automation** – Explore upcoming trends in AI-driven workflows and how to stay ahead in automation.

By the end of this book, you'll **master Zapier, eliminate repetitive tasks, and build powerful automation workflows** that will **transform the way you work**.

Now, let's dive into the world of automation!

Chapter 1: Getting Started with Zapier

1.1 Understanding No-Code Automation

The Power of No-Code Tools

The rise of no-code platforms has revolutionized the way businesses operate. No longer confined to those with programming expertise, automation is now accessible to professionals across industries. No-code tools enable users to create workflows, integrate apps, and streamline processes with simple drag-and-drop functionality. This democratization of automation empowers individuals and teams to enhance efficiency without relying on developers.

Benefits of Automation for Professionals

Automation is not just about reducing workload; it's about optimizing productivity and ensuring consistency in operations. Professionals who embrace automation can:

- Reduce time spent on repetitive tasks, allowing for more strategic work
- Minimize human error by standardizing workflows
- Improve collaboration by syncing data across tools in real time
- Increase responsiveness with automated notifications and alerts
- Enhance customer engagement by personalizing interactions

No-code automation platforms like Zapier provide these benefits without requiring complex integrations or coding knowledge.

1.2 Setting Up Your Zapier Account

Creating an Account & Exploring the Dashboard

To start using Zapier, visit the official website and sign up for an account. The setup process is straightforward:

1. Enter your email address and create a password
2. Verify your email and log in to your account

3. Choose the apps you frequently use to receive personalized automation recommendations

Once inside the dashboard, users will see a clean and intuitive interface. The primary sections include:

- **Dashboard** – The central hub where users manage workflows
- **Zaps** – A list of created automations
- **Apps** – A directory of supported applications
- **Task History** – A log of completed automation tasks

Understanding how to navigate the dashboard ensures a smooth onboarding experience.

Free vs. Paid Plans: Which One Do You Need?

Zapier offers multiple pricing plans, each catering to different levels of automation needs.

- **Free Plan** – Limited to single-step Zaps, ideal for personal use and basic automation
- **Starter Plan** – Includes multi-step Zaps, filters, and premium app integrations

- **Professional Plan** – Unlocks advanced features like conditional logic and unlimited Zaps
- **Team & Company Plans** – Designed for organizations requiring advanced security, collaboration, and API access

Selecting the right plan depends on automation complexity, business size, and the number of tasks required per month.

1.3 Core Concepts of Zapier

What are Zaps, Triggers, and Actions?

Zapier operates on a simple logic structure:

- **Zap** – An automation workflow that connects two or more applications
- **Trigger** – The event that starts the automation (e.g., receiving an email, submitting a form)
- **Action** – The task performed after the trigger occurs (e.g., adding data to a spreadsheet, sending a notification)

A single Zap consists of one trigger and at least one action.

Multi-Step Zaps Explained

While basic automation involves a single trigger-action pair, **multi-step Zaps** allow for complex workflows by chaining multiple actions. For example:

1. A customer fills out a form (Trigger)
2. The data is added to a CRM (Action 1)
3. A Slack notification is sent to the sales team (Action 2)
4. A follow-up email is scheduled (Action 3)

Multi-step Zaps eliminate the need for manual intervention, making processes seamless and efficient.

Understanding Webhooks in Zapier

For advanced users, **webhooks** provide a way to send and receive real-time data between applications that may not have native Zapier integrations. Webhooks allow users to:

- Capture incoming data from external sources
- Send data to custom applications or APIs
- Trigger workflows based on dynamic inputs

Understanding webhooks enables deeper automation possibilities, especially for IT professionals and developers looking to integrate Zapier with custom-built systems.

This foundational knowledge prepares users to start building their own automations effectively.

Chapter 2: Essential Zaps for Business Professionals

Automation can transform how professionals handle communication, project management, marketing, and sales. This chapter covers key Zapier workflows that streamline daily operations and improve efficiency.

2.1 Automating Email and Communication

Connect Gmail & Slack for Instant Alerts

In a fast-paced work environment, missing an important email can be costly. With Zapier, you can automatically send Slack notifications for critical emails.

- **Trigger:** Receive an email in Gmail with specific keywords (e.g., "urgent," "invoice," or from a VIP contact).
- **Action:** Send an alert to a designated Slack channel or direct message.

This setup ensures that teams can respond quickly to high-priority messages without constantly checking their inbox.

Automate Follow-Ups with Gmail + CRM

Timely follow-ups improve client relationships and close deals faster. Instead of manually tracking emails, automate the process with Zapier.

- **Trigger:** An email is received from a new contact.
- **Action 1:** Add the contact to a CRM (HubSpot, Salesforce, or Pipedrive).
- **Action 2:** Schedule a follow-up email after a predefined period (e.g., 3 days later).

This workflow keeps customer interactions organized and ensures no potential lead is forgotten.

Email Parsing for Automated Lead Management

Many businesses receive leads via emails, such as form submissions, inquiries, or newsletter sign-ups. Instead of manually extracting data, use email parsing automation.

- **Trigger:** A new email is received with structured data (e.g., Name, Email, Phone Number).
- **Action 1:** Parse the email using Zapier's email parser.
- **Action 2:** Add the lead information to a CRM or Google Sheets for tracking.

This automation streamlines lead collection and eliminates data entry errors.

2.2 Streamlining Project Management

Auto-Create Tasks in Trello, Asana, or Notion

Manually adding tasks to project management tools wastes time. Automate task creation by connecting Zapier with your workflow tools.

- **Trigger:** A new email is received with an assigned task.
- **Action:** Create a corresponding task in Trello, Asana, ClickUp, or Notion.

This ensures all tasks are logged without delay, keeping projects on track.

Sync Google Calendar with Project Tools

Managing deadlines across multiple platforms can be challenging. Syncing Google Calendar with project management tools keeps everything aligned.

- **Trigger:** A new event is added to Google Calendar.
- **Action:** Create a task in Asana, Monday.com, or Notion with the event details.

This workflow prevents scheduling conflicts and keeps teams updated on important deadlines.

Automate Daily Summary Reports

End-of-day reports help teams stay informed but compiling them manually can be time-consuming. Automate daily summaries to improve efficiency.

- **Trigger:** A specified time (e.g., every weekday at 6 PM).
- **Action:** Pull project updates from Notion, Asana, or Slack and send a summary email or Slack message.

This automation keeps stakeholders informed without manual effort.

2.3 Marketing & Social Media Automation

Auto-Post from RSS to Twitter, LinkedIn, and Facebook

Consistently sharing content on social media can be automated to maintain engagement without manual posting.

- **Trigger:** A new blog post is published on a website's RSS feed.
- **Action:** Automatically post the content to Twitter, LinkedIn, and Facebook with a predefined caption.

This ensures fresh content reaches your audience without delays.

Sync Leads from Facebook Ads to CRM

Manually exporting leads from Facebook Ads wastes time and risks data loss. Automate the process to keep CRM data updated in real time.

- **Trigger:** A new lead submits a form via a Facebook ad.
- **Action:** Add the lead's details to a CRM (HubSpot, Salesforce, or Zoho).

This eliminates manual data entry and ensures immediate follow-ups.

Automate Personalized Email Campaigns

Personalized email campaigns drive higher engagement, but manually segmenting and sending emails is inefficient.

- **Trigger:** A new contact is added to a CRM or email list.
- **Action:** Enroll the contact in an automated email sequence with tailored messaging.

This workflow nurtures leads and maintains customer engagement with minimal effort.

2.4 Sales & Customer Relationship Management

Automate Lead Capture from Forms (Google Forms, Typeform, etc.)

Instead of manually collecting and inputting lead data, automate lead capture from form submissions.

- **Trigger:** A new response is submitted via Google Forms, Typeform, or JotForm.
- **Action:** Add the lead's details to a CRM or Google Sheets.

This ensures that every lead is logged and ready for follow-up.

Sync New Contacts to CRM (HubSpot, Salesforce, Pipedrive)

Keeping contact databases up to date manually is inefficient. Automate the process by syncing new contacts across platforms.

- **Trigger:** A new contact is added to Google Contacts, Outlook, or a lead form.
- **Action:** Create a new record in a CRM (HubSpot, Salesforce, Pipedrive).

This automation ensures sales teams always have the latest contact information.

Automate Sales Reporting

Manually compiling sales reports can be tedious and prone to errors. Automate data collection and reporting for accurate insights.

- **Trigger:** A new sale is recorded in an e-commerce platform (Shopify, WooCommerce, Stripe).
- **Action:** Update a sales report in Google Sheets or generate a summary email.

Automating reports provides real-time business insights without the need for manual tracking.

Chapter 3: Advanced Zapier Workflows

For professionals looking to optimize automation beyond basic Zaps, advanced features like multi-step workflows, webhooks, and data transformation provide powerful capabilities. This chapter explores how to build smarter, more efficient automations.

3.1 Multi-Step Zaps & Conditional Logic

How to Use Paths for Smart Decision-Making

In complex workflows, different actions may be required based on specific conditions. Zapier's Paths feature allows users to create multiple outcomes within a single Zap.

- **Example Use Case:**
  - A lead fills out a form with different service requests.
  - **Path 1:** If they select "Enterprise Support," create a HubSpot lead and notify the sales team.

o **Path 2:** If they select "Standard Support," add them to a Mailchimp nurture campaign.

By using Paths, businesses can automate decision-making based on predefined criteria, ensuring customized responses for different scenarios.

Delays & Filters to Optimize Workflows

Not all actions should occur immediately. Delays and filters help refine automation processes for better timing and efficiency.

- **Delays:** Useful for scheduling follow-ups, sending reminders, or spacing out actions.
    - o Example: Delay a Slack notification until 9 AM on the next business day.
- **Filters:** Prevent unnecessary Zaps from running unless conditions are met.
    - o Example: Only process a customer support request if the email subject contains "urgent."

Using delays and filters reduces clutter, prevents redundant actions, and improves workflow efficiency.

3.2 Working with Webhooks & APIs

Understanding Webhooks for Advanced Integrations

Webhooks allow apps to communicate in real time, even when they don't have direct Zapier integrations. With webhooks, users can send or receive data from external applications.

- **Example Use Case:**
    - A new order is placed in an e-commerce platform that doesn't natively integrate with Zapier.
    - A webhook triggers an API call to fetch order details.
    - The order information is then sent to a CRM or inventory system.

By leveraging webhooks, businesses can integrate custom applications without waiting for official Zapier support.

How to Connect Non-Native Apps

If an app isn't directly supported by Zapier, APIs can bridge the gap. Using **Zapier Webhooks + API Requests**, users can:

- **Pull data** from an external source (e.g., retrieve customer details from a custom database).
- **Send data** to an external platform (e.g., update an order status in an ERP system).

This flexibility expands the range of automation possibilities beyond Zapier's built-in app directory.

3.3 Data Formatting & Transformation

Use Zapier Formatter to Clean & Modify Data

Raw data from different sources often requires formatting before being useful. The Zapier Formatter tool helps process data by:

- Extracting specific information from text (e.g., pulling a phone number from an email).
- Converting all text to uppercase or lowercase for consistency.

- Splitting full names into first and last name fields.

Automating data formatting ensures accuracy and prevents manual data cleaning.

Convert Text, Numbers, and Dates Automatically

Different platforms store data in various formats, requiring conversion for compatibility. Zapier can automate these transformations:

- **Text Conversion:** Remove special characters, extract values, or format capitalization.
- **Number Formatting:** Convert currency values, apply mathematical calculations, or round decimals.
- **Date Standardization:** Change date formats across time zones or applications.

By automating data processing, professionals can ensure seamless integration between different platforms.

Chapter 4: Industry-Specific Automation Strategies

Automation needs vary across industries, and Zapier provides tailored solutions for different professional fields. Whether you are an entrepreneur, HR professional, financial expert, or developer, this chapter explores how to implement automation to improve efficiency and reduce manual work.

4.1 Zapier for Entrepreneurs & Small Businesses

Small businesses often operate with lean teams, making automation a crucial tool for maximizing efficiency. Zapier helps entrepreneurs streamline financial tasks, customer interactions, and business operations.

Automate Invoicing & Payment Reminders

Timely invoicing is essential for maintaining healthy cash flow, but manual invoicing can be time-consuming. Automating invoice generation and payment reminders ensures accuracy and improves collection rates.

- **Zapier Workflow Example:**
  - **Trigger:** A new order is placed in Shopify, Stripe, or PayPal.
  - **Action 1:** Automatically generate an invoice in QuickBooks, Xero, or FreshBooks.
  - **Action 2:** Send the invoice to the customer via email.
  - **Action 3:** If payment is not received within 7 days, send a follow-up reminder.

By automating this process, businesses reduce administrative workload and minimize late payments.

Sync Accounting Data to QuickBooks & Xero

Keeping financial records up-to-date is critical for tax reporting and business insights. Manually entering transaction data can lead to errors, but Zapier allows seamless data synchronization.

- **Zapier Workflow Example:**
  - **Trigger:** A new payment is received via PayPal or Stripe.

- Action: Automatically log the transaction into QuickBooks or Xero.

With real-time financial updates, businesses can maintain accurate books without manual data entry.

4.2 Zapier for HR & Recruiting

Human resource management involves repetitive administrative tasks such as job tracking, employee onboarding, and performance management. Zapier helps HR professionals automate workflows, improving efficiency and candidate experience.

Automate Job Application Tracking

Recruiting involves handling numerous applications, resumes, and emails. Manually tracking each application can be overwhelming, but Zapier can automatically organize applications in a structured format.

- **Zapier Workflow Example:**
  - **Trigger:** A candidate submits an application through LinkedIn, Indeed, or a company website.

- Action 1: Add candidate details to an Airtable or Google Sheets tracker.
- Action 2: Notify the hiring manager via Slack or email.
- Action 3: Send an automated acknowledgment email to the candidate.

With this system in place, HR teams can streamline recruitment without losing track of potential hires.

Streamline Employee Onboarding with Zapier

New employee onboarding requires multiple steps, including account setup, document submission, and HR system updates. Automating these steps enhances efficiency and ensures compliance.

- **Zapier Workflow Example:**
  - **Trigger:** A new hire is added to an HR system (BambooHR, Workday, or Google Sheets).
  - **Action 1:** Send a welcome email with onboarding documents.

- o **Action 2:** Create an account for the employee in Slack, Notion, or Microsoft Teams.
- o **Action 3:** Schedule an introductory meeting on Google Calendar.

Automating onboarding ensures a smooth and consistent experience for every new employee.

4.3 Zapier for Finance & Accounting

Financial professionals rely on accurate data tracking and timely reporting. Zapier helps automate key finance functions, reducing manual data entry and improving decision-making.

Automate Expense Tracking & Approval

Processing expense reports manually can be inefficient and prone to delays. With Zapier, finance teams can automatically capture and approve expenses.

- **Zapier Workflow Example:**
  - o **Trigger:** An employee submits an expense report via Google Forms or Expensify.

- Action 1: Add the expense to a Google Sheet or accounting software.
- Action 2: Notify the finance team via Slack or email.
- Action 3: If the expense exceeds a set amount, trigger an approval request.

This system speeds up approvals and ensures financial records are always up to date.

Sync Bank Transactions to Google Sheets

For financial reporting and reconciliation, having real-time transaction records is crucial. Manually copying transactions is inefficient, but Zapier can automatically sync banking data.

- **Zapier Workflow Example:**
  - **Trigger:** A new transaction appears in a bank feed (Plaid, PayPal, Stripe).
  - **Action:** Log the transaction in a Google Sheet or financial dashboard.

This automation keeps finance teams updated with real-time financial insights.

4.4 Zapier for IT & Developers

IT professionals and developers handle complex workflows involving system monitoring, notifications, and integrations. Zapier can automate these tasks, reducing manual intervention and improving response times.

Automate GitHub Issues & Notifications

Managing GitHub issues and pull requests manually can slow down software development. Automating notifications and tracking ensures teams stay informed.

- **Zapier Workflow Example:**
    - **Trigger:** A new issue is created in GitHub.
    - **Action 1:** Notify the team in Slack or Microsoft Teams.
    - **Action 2:** Add the issue to a Trello or Jira board.
    - **Action 3:** Send an email alert if the issue is labeled "urgent."

With automated notifications, development teams can respond faster and improve collaboration.

Connect APIs for Custom Integrations

Not all apps integrate directly with Zapier, but developers can use webhooks and APIs to automate workflows.

- **Zapier Workflow Example:**
  - **Trigger:** A webhook receives data from a custom application.
  - **Action:** Send the data to a third-party service (e.g., log customer behavior into a CRM).

This flexibility allows IT teams to connect any application and automate complex workflows.

Conclusion

Every industry can benefit from automation, but the key to success is implementing the right workflows for specific business needs. Whether you're an entrepreneur, HR manager, finance professional, or developer, Zapier provides tools to streamline operations, enhance efficiency, and reduce manual tasks.

Chapter 5: Troubleshooting & Optimization

While Zapier simplifies automation, users may occasionally encounter issues with failed workflows, authentication errors, or excessive task usage. This chapter provides practical solutions to common problems and strategies to optimize performance and reduce costs.

5.1 Common Zapier Errors & How to Fix Them

Understanding the most frequent Zapier issues can help users troubleshoot problems quickly and keep workflows running smoothly.

Authentication Issues & API Limits

Many Zapier integrations require authentication with third-party apps, and issues can arise due to expired tokens, incorrect credentials, or API rate limits.

Common Causes & Fixes:

- **Expired Authentication Tokens:** Some apps, like Google or Facebook, require periodic reauthorization.
  - **Fix:** Reconnect the app under "My Apps" in Zapier and update permissions.
- **Incorrect API Credentials:** When using APIs or webhooks, incorrect keys can cause authentication failures.
  - **Fix:** Double-check API keys and ensure they have the correct permissions.
- **API Rate Limits:** Some services impose limits on how many API requests Zapier can send in a given period.
  - **Fix:** Reduce the frequency of Zaps or batch requests when possible.

Troubleshooting Failed Zaps

Zaps can fail for various reasons, from incorrect data formatting to temporary service outages.

Steps to Diagnose & Fix Failed Zaps:

1. **Check Zap History:** Go to the "Task History" tab to identify failed runs and review error messages.
2. **Verify Input Data:** Ensure trigger data is structured correctly. For example, a date field in one app may not match the required format in another.
3. **Use Zapier Formatter:** If the issue is data-related, use the Formatter tool to clean or modify the data before passing it to the next step.
4. **Re-test the Zap:** Run a manual test from the Zap editor to confirm that each step works correctly.
5. **Check Third-Party App Status:** If an app's API is down or undergoing maintenance, wait and retry later.

5.2 Performance Optimization & Cost Management

Since Zapier charges based on task usage, optimizing workflows can help reduce costs while improving efficiency.

How to Reduce Zapier Task Usage

Each step in a Zap counts as a task, and excessive or unnecessary steps can lead to higher costs.

Optimization Strategies:

- **Use Filters to Prevent Unnecessary Task Execution:**
    o Example: If a Zap triggers on every email received, add a filter to process only emails with specific keywords.
- **Leverage Paths Instead of Multiple Zaps:**
    o Instead of creating multiple Zaps for different conditions, use Paths to create conditional logic in a single Zap.
- **Use Delay & Batch Actions:**
    o Instead of processing tasks in real time, batch them to reduce API calls and task usage.
- **Automate with Webhooks Instead of Polling Triggers:**
    o Some apps allow real-time triggers using webhooks instead of scheduled polling, which saves Zapier tasks.

Best Practices for Keeping Zaps Efficient

- **Use Multi-Step Zaps Efficiently:** Plan workflows to minimize redundant actions.
- **Avoid Duplicate Triggers:** Ensure a Zap doesn't trigger multiple times for the same event.
- **Regularly Review & Optimize Workflows:** Periodically audit Zaps to remove outdated or unnecessary steps.

Conclusion

By troubleshooting common issues and optimizing workflows, professionals can ensure their Zapier automations run smoothly and cost-effectively. The next chapter will explore advanced customization techniques for even greater flexibility and power.

Chapter 6: Future Trends in Automation & AI Integration

As automation continues to evolve, the integration of artificial intelligence (AI) with no-code tools like Zapier is reshaping how businesses operate. This chapter explores the role of AI in automation, emerging AI-powered Zapier integrations, and how professionals can take their automation strategies beyond Zapier.

6.1 The Role of AI in No-Code Automation

AI-driven automation is transforming the way professionals handle repetitive tasks, decision-making, and workflow optimization. No-code automation platforms like Zapier are beginning to integrate AI capabilities, making workflows more intelligent and efficient.

Key Benefits of AI-Driven Automation:

- **Smarter Decision-Making:** AI-powered Zaps can analyze data and make real-time decisions without manual intervention.

- **Enhanced Data Processing:** AI tools can extract insights from unstructured data like emails, documents, and customer feedback.

- **Improved Customer Engagement:** AI-driven chatbots, sentiment analysis, and predictive analytics can enhance customer interactions.

- **Workflow Optimization:** AI can detect inefficiencies and suggest automation improvements based on usage patterns.

Use Cases of AI in No-Code Automation:

- **AI-Powered Email Parsing:** Automatically extract key information from emails and categorize responses.

- **AI Sentiment Analysis for Customer Support:** Use AI to analyze customer messages and route them to the right team.

- **AI-Generated Content Automation:** Automatically create and distribute content across social media and marketing platforms.

6.2 Emerging Zapier Integrations for AI-Powered Workflows

Zapier is expanding its integrations with AI-based tools, enabling professionals to build smarter workflows. Some of the most powerful AI integrations available on Zapier include:

1. AI Text & Content Generation

- **ChatGPT & OpenAI Integration:** Automate content creation, customer support replies, or brainstorming ideas.
- **Grammarly & AI Writing Assistants:** Enhance automated emails, reports, or blog drafts before publishing.

2. AI-Powered Customer Support & Chatbots

- **Intercom + AI Sentiment Analysis:** Route support tickets based on sentiment and urgency.
- **Drift + Zapier:** Automate chatbot interactions and CRM updates.

3. AI for Data Analysis & Prediction

- **MonkeyLearn + Zapier:** Use AI to classify and extract meaning from customer feedback.
- **Google AI & AutoML Integration:** Automate predictive analytics for business forecasting.

4. AI Image & Video Processing

- **Synthesia AI Video Generation:** Automate video creation for marketing and training.
- **DeepL AI Translation:** Automatically translate documents and customer inquiries in multiple languages.

6.3 Next Steps: Expanding Beyond Zapier While Zapier is a powerful no-code automation tool, professionals looking for even more advanced AI-powered automation may want to explore additional platforms.

1. AI-Powered No-Code Alternatives to Zapier

- **Make (formerly Integromat):** Offers more complex logic-based automation with AI-enhanced workflows.
- **n8n.io:** Open-source workflow automation with customizable AI integrations.
- **Microsoft Power Automate:** AI-driven automation with deep integration into the Microsoft ecosystem.

2. Custom AI Automation with Low-Code & API Tools

For professionals with some technical expertise, low-code platforms can provide more flexibility:

- **Bubble.io + AI Plugins:** Build AI-powered web apps with no coding required.
- **Python + Zapier Webhooks:** Combine custom AI models with Zapier workflows.

- **Google Cloud Functions & AWS Lambda:** Run AI-powered automation scripts beyond Zapier's limitations.

3. The Future of AI-Driven Automation

Looking ahead, AI will continue to redefine automation. Some key trends include:

- **Self-Learning AI Workflows:** AI will predict and optimize automation rules dynamically.
- **Voice-Activated Automation:** AI assistants like Alexa and Google Assistant will trigger workflows via voice commands.
- **AI-Driven Process Mining:** AI will analyze business workflows and suggest improvements automatically.

AI-powered automation is the future, and professionals leveraging Zapier and emerging AI integrations will stay ahead of the competition. By combining AI with no-code tools, businesses can streamline operations, enhance decision-making, and unlock new efficiencies.

Conclusion & Resources

Recap & Key Takeaways

Automation is no longer just a convenience—it's a necessity for professionals looking to improve efficiency, save time, and scale their operations. This guide has provided a deep dive into Zapier's capabilities, from basic automations to advanced AI-driven workflows.

Key Takeaways:

1. **No-Code Automation is a Game Changer:** Professionals from all industries can leverage Zapier to streamline tasks without needing coding expertise.

2. **Multi-Step Zaps Unlock Advanced Productivity:** By chaining multiple actions together, businesses can create powerful automated workflows.

3. **AI is the Future of Automation:** Integrating AI-powered tools with Zapier can enhance data processing, customer engagement, and predictive analytics.

4. **Optimization Matters:** Reducing Zap usage, troubleshooting errors, and ensuring workflows run efficiently can save both time and costs.

5. **Beyond Zapier:** Exploring alternative automation tools and low-code platforms can further extend automation possibilities.

By implementing the strategies outlined in this guide, professionals can transform repetitive manual tasks into efficient, automated workflows.

Additional Zapier Learning Resources

To deepen your knowledge and stay updated on Zapier's latest features, here are some key learning resources:

Official Zapier Resources:

- **Zapier Help Center:** zapier.com/help – Comprehensive guides, troubleshooting tips, and FAQs.
- **Zapier University:** zapier.com/learn – Free courses on automation and workflow optimization.

- **Zapier Community:** community.zapier.com – A forum for automation enthusiasts to share workflows and solutions.

Recommended Books & Blogs:

- *Automate Your Busywork* by Aytekin Tank – A practical guide to using automation for productivity.
- *The No-Code Revolution* by Alex Galea – Insights into the growing no-code ecosystem, including Zapier.
- **Zapier Blog:** zapier.com/blog – Case studies, automation strategies, and AI trends.

YouTube & Online Courses:

- **Zapier YouTube Channel:** YouTube.com/Zapier – Tutorials and use-case demonstrations.
- **Udemy & Coursera Courses:** Search for "Zapier Automation" for in-depth online training.

Exclusive Automation Templates & Case Studies

Pre-Built Zapier Templates:

To help you get started quickly, here are some essential automation templates:

1. **Lead Management:** Google Forms → CRM – Automatically add new form responses to HubSpot, Salesforce, or Pipedrive.
2. **Marketing Automation:** RSS Feed → Social Media – Auto-post new blog articles to LinkedIn, Twitter, and Facebook.
3. **Project Management:** Gmail → Trello/Asana – Convert emails into tasks for better workflow tracking.
4. **Finance & Accounting:** Stripe → QuickBooks – Sync Stripe payments with accounting software.

Real-World Case Studies:

1. Automating Client Onboarding for a Marketing Agency

- Challenge: Manually managing new client intake was time-consuming.

- Solution: Using Zapier to connect Typeform, Slack, and Trello for seamless onboarding.
- Result: Reduced onboarding time by 60%, improving client satisfaction.

2. AI-Powered Customer Support for an E-Commerce Store

- Challenge: High volume of repetitive customer inquiries.
- Solution: AI-driven sentiment analysis (MonkeyLearn + Zapier) to categorize tickets automatically.
- Result: Faster response times and improved customer service efficiency.

3. Automating Job Applicant Tracking for HR Teams

- Challenge: Manually screening resumes and updating spreadsheets.
- Solution: Using Zapier to extract resumes from emails and add structured data to Google Sheets.
- Result: Streamlined recruitment process and saved hours of manual work.

Final Words

Automation is not just about saving time—it's about enabling professionals to focus on high-value tasks that drive growth and innovation. By leveraging Zapier and AI-driven workflows, businesses can enhance productivity, streamline operations, and stay ahead in an increasingly automated world.

Now it's your turn to take action. Experiment with Zapier, optimize your workflows, and embrace the future of automation. The possibilities are endless!

Table of Contents

Zapier for Automation:...1

A Professional's Guide to Streamlining Workflows.........1

Introduction...1

    Why Automation Matters in 2025.................................1

    What is Zapier? (Overview & Core Features)...............3

        Key Features of Zapier:..3

    Who This Guide is For...4

    How to Use This Book...6

Chapter 1: Getting Started with Zapier.............................8

    1.1 Understanding No-Code Automation........................8

        The Power of No-Code Tools...............................8

        Benefits of Automation for Professionals........8

    1.2 Setting Up Your Zapier Account................................9

        Creating an Account & Exploring the Dashboard.......9

        Free vs. Paid Plans: Which One Do You Need?.........10

    1.3 Core Concepts of Zapier...11

        What are Zaps, Triggers, and Actions?...............11

        Multi-Step Zaps Explained..................................12

        Understanding Webhooks in Zapier...................12

Chapter 2: Essential Zaps for Business Professionals....14

    2.1 Automating Email and Communication...................14

        Connect Gmail & Slack for Instant Alerts.................14

        Automate Follow-Ups with Gmail + CRM.................15

        Email Parsing for Automated Lead Management......15

    2.2 Streamlining Project Management...........................16

Auto-Create Tasks in Trello, Asana, or Notion 16

Sync Google Calendar with Project Tools 17

Automate Daily Summary Reports 17

2.3 Marketing & Social Media Automation 18

Auto-Post from RSS to Twitter, LinkedIn, and
Facebook..18

Sync Leads from Facebook Ads to CRM.....................18

Automate Personalized Email Campaigns 19

2.4 Sales & Customer Relationship Management 19

Automate Lead Capture from Forms (Google Forms,
Typeform, etc.)..19

Sync New Contacts to CRM (HubSpot, Salesforce,
Pipedrive) 20

Automate Sales Reporting 21

Chapter 3: Advanced Zapier Workflows 22

3.1 Multi-Step Zaps & Conditional Logic 22

How to Use Paths for Smart Decision-Making...........22

Delays & Filters to Optimize Workflows.....................23

3.2 Working with Webhooks & APIs...............................24

Understanding Webhooks for Advanced Integrations
....24

How to Connect Non-Native Apps..............................25

3.3 Data Formatting & Transformation 25

Use Zapier Formatter to Clean & Modify Data...........25

Convert Text, Numbers, and Dates Automatically...26

Chapter 4: Industry-Specific Automation Strategies......27

4.1 Zapier for Entrepreneurs & Small Businesses........27

Automate Invoicing & Payment Reminders.............27

Sync Accounting Data to QuickBooks & Xero 28

4.2 Zapier for HR & Recruiting.............................29

Automate Job Application Tracking.....................29

Streamline Employee Onboarding with Zapier..........30

4.3 Zapier for Finance & Accounting 31

Automate Expense Tracking & Approval..................31

Sync Bank Transactions to Google Sheets 32

4.4 Zapier for IT & Developers.............................33

Automate GitHub Issues & Notifications...................33

Connect APIs for Custom Integrations 34

Conclusion 34

Chapter 5: Troubleshooting & Optimization 35

5.1 Common Zapier Errors & How to Fix Them...........35

Authentication Issues & API Limits 35

Troubleshooting Failed Zaps.............................36

5.2 Performance Optimization & Cost Management...37

How to Reduce Zapier Task Usage.......................38

Best Practices for Keeping Zaps Efficient.................39

Conclusion 39

Chapter 6: Future Trends in Automation & AI
Integration..40

6.1 The Role of AI in No-Code Automation 40

Key Benefits of AI-Driven Automation:....................41

Use Cases of AI in No-Code Automation:.................41

6.2 Emerging Zapier Integrations for AI-Powered Workflows...42

   1. AI Text & Content Generation...................................42

   2. AI-Powered Customer Support & Chatbots............43

   3. AI for Data Analysis & Prediction...........................43

   4. AI Image & Video Processing....................................43

6.3 Next Steps: Expanding Beyond Zapier While Zapier is a powerful no-code automation tool, professionals looking for even more advanced AI-powered automation may want to explore additional platforms. 43

   1. AI-Powered No-Code Alternatives to Zapier..........44

   2. Custom AI Automation with Low-Code & API Tools..44

   3. The Future of AI-Driven Automation........................45

Conclusion & Resources 46

   Recap & Key Takeaways 46

   Key Takeaways: 46

Additional Zapier Learning Resources...........................47

   Official Zapier Resources: 47

   Recommended Books & Blogs:.......................................48

   YouTube & Online Courses:...48

Exclusive Automation Templates & Case Studies........49

   Pre-Built Zapier Templates:...49

   Real-World Case Studies:...49

Final Words...51